Copyright@2018 Sumita Mukherjee. All rights reserved. No part of this book may be distributed, reproduced, stored in retrieval system or transmitted in any form or by any means, electronic, mechanical, recording or otherwise, without written permission from the copyright holder. For information regarding permission, please contact wizkidsclub.com

www.wizkidsclub.com

Author: Sumita Mukherjee

First Edition: March 2018

All rights reserved @Sumita Mukherjee 2018

Table of Contents

Introduction 4
Engineering Design Process 5
Material List 6
Marine Biologist 7
Aeronautics Engineer 10
Mechanical Engineer 16
Electrical Engineer 19
Chemical Engineer 23
Civil Engineer 27
Acoustical Engineer 31
NASA Scientist 35
Toy Designer 38
Maker Showcase 41

Introduction: How Do People Invent Things?

People from every corner of the world, of different ages, with different levels of education invent by finding out problems, using creative ideas, and developing new solutions. Inventor's and engineers initial ideas rarely solve a problem. Instead they try different ideas, learn from mistakes, and try again, There are a series of steps they use to arrive at a solution and it is called the Engineering Design Process. As you work through your invention process, use the guide below to understand the invention process and tie it to specific steps of the Engineering design process.

Five steps that can help you to invent something new

ASK:
- What are some different ways to tackle today's problem? Brainstorm ideas.
- How creative can we be? Off-the-wall suggestions often spark GREAT ideas!

IMAGINE:
- Which brainstormed ideas are really possible given our time, tools, and materials? Choose the idea that seems to work the best.

PLAN:
- Design and sketch out your idea.
- What materials will you need to build your invention?
- Come up with the step-by-step process in order to build it.

CREATE:
- Build it using the plan and the materials. Test it out and see what works and what doesn't.

IMPROVE:
- What do you think is the best features of your invention? Why?
- If you had more time, how could you improve your invention?

Both inventors and engineers look for ways to improve things in areas like health, food, safety, transportation, aerospace, electronics, communication, and the environment. How about you try your own?

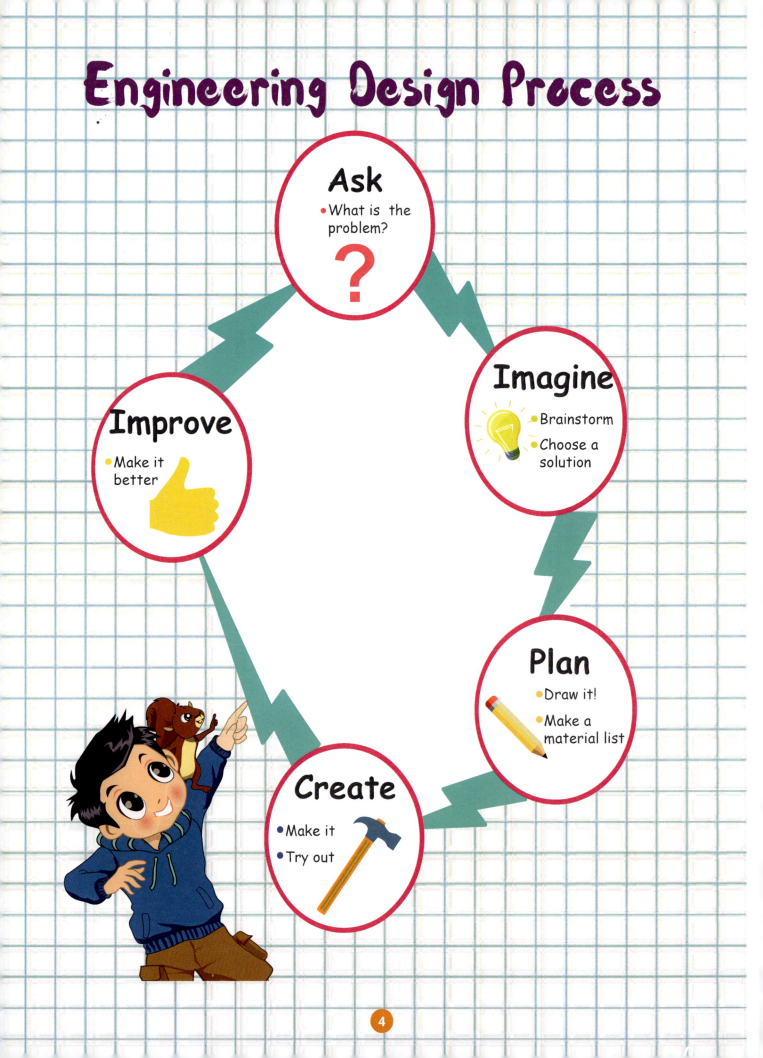

Materials List: STEAM Program

1. wooden blocks
2. magnetic tiles
3. paper rolls
4. aluminium foil
5. corks
6. nuts and bolts
7. bottles
8. sponges
9. Tupperware
10. curlers
11. books
12. pipe cleaners
13. rocks
14. cups
15. flooring tiles
16. carpet samples
17. pasta
18. spools
19. wire
20. sugar cubes
21. foam
22. LEGOs
23. toothpicks
24. grapes
25. marshmallows
26. clay
27. gumdrops
28. raisins
29. bluetack
30. wax
31. play dough
32. cheese
33. jelly beans
34. glow sticks
35. straws
36. tape
37. kids :)
38. chalk
39. toy train tracks
40. sticks
41. crackers
42. cans
43. playing cards
44. snow
45. ice
46. pillows
47. popsicle sticks
48. pool noodles
49. bubbles
50. kinetic sand
51. balloons
52. cotton swabs
53. beads
54. party horns
55. marble runs
56. plastic caps
57. index cards
58. plexiglass
59. toilet paper
60. spice jars
61. rain gutters
62. yogurt cups
63. egg cartons
64. silk flowers
65. bricks
66. coffee pods
67. foil baking tins
68. candy hearts
69. salt dough
70. pinecones
71. tubing
72. greeting cards
73. wood pieces
74. packing peanuts
75. foam cubes
76. cd cases
77. PVC pipe
78. circuits
79. dowel rods
80. bowls
81. magnets
82. milk cartons
83. pots & pans
84. plants
85. bark
86. coffee cans
87. wired ribbon
88. chip tubes
89. foam tiles
90. packing peanuts
91. paper mache
92. floral wire
93. berry baskets
94. plaster of paris
95. M&M tubes
96. plastick forks
97. tree branches
98. hair clips
99. crates

100. your creativity!

Career Introduction: Marine Biologist

 Engineering connection: Engineers use various techniques to provide speedy solutions to oil spills or other threats to natural water resources. A Marine Biologist is a scientist who studies and protects the animals and plants that live in the ocean.

Grade level: 1-5
Time: 60 minutes

Summary: Engineers use various techniques to provide speedy solutions to oil spills. Students work in teams to analyse an "oil spill" in the classroom, then remove the oil from the water. Students use everyday items to build their oil clean-up system, evaluate and present their findings to the class.

OIL SPILL CLEANUP!

Learning objectives:

Learn about environmental engineering and chemical engineering. Learn about engineering design, planning and construction.

RELEVANT STANDARDS:

National Science Education Standards Grades K-4
Standards for Technological Literacy

Materials:

Water basin or sink to represent the ocean/sea
1/2 cup vegetable oil mixed with cocoa powder to create the crude oil
Jar
Feathers
Plastic birds and sea animals
One set of materials for each group of students:
Rubber bands, paper towels, string, toothpicks, cotton balls, plastic wrap, popsicle sticks, pipette, cardboard, spoon, other items as needed.

With the Students:

ASK (5 min):

Get students interested by telling them that a marine biologist is a scientist who studies and protects the animals and plants that live in the ocean. Show a picture of a marine biologist.

IMAGINE (10 min):

Explain that marine biologists find ways to make sure the ocean stays clean for animals to live in. Sometimes big ships carrying oil meet with an accident and spill the oil. This is bad for the animals and plants. Today they are going to be marine biologists.

Students must work as a team to design a system to clean up an oil spill. The cocoa/vegetable oil mix, representing the oil spill, is poured into a container of water, such as a water trough, large bucket or sink.

PLAN (10 minutes):

Students meet and develop a plan to firstly contain the oil and then to remove it. They can select from the materials provided to serve as their tools. Student teams will describe their plan both in writing and with a diagram and then present their plan to the class. Plans may be altered after feedback from others during the presentation stage.

Students then proceed to execute their plan and marks can be scored based on how "clean" the water is after the clean-up process is complete.

CREATE (25 minutes):

Start by filling the sink with water. Add the plastic animals and feathers to represent the sea creatures.

Mix together the cocoa powder and vegetable oil and add that to the water. Encourage the students to execute their plan and remove the oil from water. Spoons can be used to scoop out the spill, paper towels to absorb it or students can create a suction device or chemical reactions to absorb the oil.

 IMPROVE (10 minutes):

Make a chart of the different methods explorers used to remove the oil. Note down which methods worked best.
1. Did you succeed in removing all the oil from the "oil spill?"
2. If your system failed, what do you think went wrong?
3. Describe a system another student team created that you thought worked well. What did they do differently?
4. Did you decide to revise your plan while actually doing the containment or clean-up? Why? How?

PROJECT EXTENSION:

Write and draw the condition of feathers and birds when they are soaked in oil. How can engineers design better hulls on ships, so that there is no oil spill in the event of a ship wreck?

Career Introduction: Aeronautics Engineer

 Engineering connection: Aeronautics Engineers design and build an airplane or other flying machine.

Grade level: 1-5
Time: 60 minutes

Summary: In this lesson, teams of students will learn about basic aerodynamics by constructing a rocket from a balloon propelled along a guide-string. For older kids, they use this model to learn about Newton's laws of motion. They will also examine the effect of different balloon sizes on the motion of the rocket.

BALLOON ROCKETS

Learning objectives:

After doing this activity, students should be able to:
- Understand practical applications of Newton's Laws of Motion.
- Use the model of the balloon to understand the different forces that act on the rocket.
- Collect data from the experiment and graph the results.

 RELEVANT STANDARDS:

National Science Education Standards: Physical Science: Properties of Objects and Materials, Motions and Forces, Science as Inquiry: Abilities necessary to do scientific inquiry, Science and Technology Standard: Understanding about Science and Technology Standards for Technology Literacy:

The Nature of Technology. Students will develop an understanding of the role of troubleshooting, research and development, invention and innovation, and experimentation in problem solivng.

The Designed World. Students will develop an understanding of and be able to select and use transportation technologies.

Knowledge gained from other fields of study has a direct effect on the development of technological products and systems.

Materials:

Plastic drinking straw
25 ft. of fishing line (20-50g weight) or string (nylon [slippery] string works better than twine [rough])
Long, tube-shaped balloon
Tape measure or meter stick

ASK (5 min):

Get students interested by asking, "Do you think you can make a balloon rocket that can go from one side of the room to the other along a string?". Tell students that Aeronautics Engineers design and build an airplane or other flying machine. Today they will be build a rocket like an aeronautic engineer. They will need to make 3 balloons (small, medium and large) and measure the distance travelled by each.

IMAGINE (10 min):

Start with an in-class demonstration. For example, have a student or the teacher stand on a skateboard and throw a ball. What happens? Have a student or the teacher throw a ball filled with lead weights or similar, very heavy object (this could be dangerous; be very careful not to fall). What happens? (Answer: The student or teacher rolls backwards on the skateboard.) For more than 2,000 years, rockets and rocket-propelled flight has been in use. Ancient China used gunpowder to make fireworks and rockets. People have gained a scientific understanding of how rockets work in the past 300 years. Now a days, aerospace engineers make rockets fly farther, faster, higher and with more accurately. Sir Isaac Newton's three laws of motion helps us understand how rockets work. It is important for engineers to understand Newton's laws because they not only describe how rockets work, they explain how everything that moves or stays still works! (Use images and relevant content according to the grade level)

PLAN (10 minutes):

Have kids plan out and discuss how they would make the 3 balloons move along the string. Ask them to sketch their designs on a piece of paper or in their design notebooks. Prompt them to tie the string between to chairs at a distance or use door knobs.

CREATE (25 minutes):

Now have the kids begin making it.

1. Thread the string through the straw.
2. Tie each end of the string to a chair, and pull the chairs apart so that the string is taut.
3. Now blow one balloon of small size. Close the balloon end with finger. No air should escape.
4. Tape a drinking straw on the balloon.
5. Count down to zero, and let go of the balloon. . . ZOOMMM!
6. Have students measure the distance their balloon rocket traveled on the string and complete the worksheet.
7. Now blow a medium balloon and repeat the experiment.
8. Record the distance travelled by the medium sized balloon.
9. Repeat the experiment with the large sized balloon and record the distance travelled.

While waiting for other students to finish their worksheets, students with completed worksheets should compare their answers with their peers.
Review and discuss the worksheet answers with students.

👍 IMPROVE (10 minutes):

Discuss what happened. Have kids talk about their designs. Then they discuss their worksheets results. Which balooon went the furthest? What can you do it make it move further?

Ask the students to write a journal entry on how the balloon rocket experiment could relate to something else they've encountered. Why are Newton's laws of motion so important in our world?

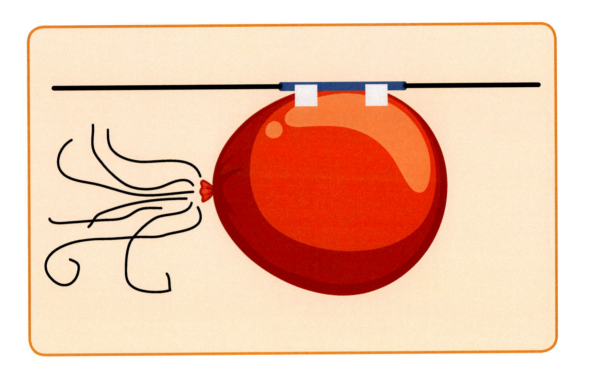

📁 PROJECT EXTENSION:

Have the students re-engineer their balloon rockets again, adding extra features to make the balloon go further. Allow them to use more straw and tape, and more than one balloon. Conduct a race to see which engineering team built the best balloon rocket. Ask that team to explain why their design worked as it did, in terms of Newton's three laws of motion (Depends on the grade level).

Name: _____   Date: _____

Action-Reaction! Activity – Worksheet

1. Draw a picture of your "Action-Reaction Rocket." Label the action and reaction forces.

2. Are the action and reaction forces equal, less than or greater than each other?

3. Predict the distance traveled along the string for a balloon that is filled with air so that it is small, medium and large in size. Then, record the actual distances traveled during three trials for each size balloon.

Balloon Size	Trial #	Predicted Distance	Actual Distance Travelled
Small	1		
	2		
	3		
Medium	1		
	2		
	3		
Large	1		
	2		
	3		

4. How does the balloon size relate to the action and reaction forces?

5. Graph the results with the size of balloon on the x-axis and the distance traveled on the y-axis.

Career Introduction: Mechanical Engineer

 Engineering connection: Machines come in many sizes, from massive ones like cranes and trucks to nano-sized tools. Mechanical engineers are people who design, build and maintain them all.

Grade level: 1-5
Time: 60 minutes

Summary: In this lesson, teams of students will explore the engineering design process by modifying a paper cup to carry a marble down a zipline. They will learn to brainstorm, test, evaluate and redesign their devices to improve accuracy.

ZIPPING ZIPLINE

Learning objectives:

Work in cooperative groups to follow the engineering design process and understand which parts of their design proved key in getting the marble to hit the target.
Newton's laws of motion.
(According to grade)

RELEVANT STANDARDS:

National Science Education Standards
International Technology Education Association Content Standards
National Council of Teachers of Mathematics Standards

Materials:

2–4 small paper cups
Marble ball
3-4 plastic straws
Scissors
Single-hole punch
5 feet of smooth line (e.g., fishing line or unwaxed dental floss)
Tape (duct or masking)
   Weights such as small rocks or washers

With the Students:

ASK (5 min):

Get students interested by telling them that a mechanical engineer is a person who designs and maintains machines. From roller coasters to cranes, they can build anything. Today students will be making a zipline that can carry a marble and hit a target.

IMAGINE (10 min):

Have students imagine and discuss what a zipline is. How can a zipline be made? Have them look at some images of cable cars, or videos of zipline games. That way they have better understanding of the problem.

PLAN (10 minutes):

Look at your materials and think through how you can use them to build a zipline carrier. Then sketch your ideas on a piece of paper or in your design notebook.
1. Using these materials, what carrier can you design that can carry a marble ball down a zipline?
2. How will you make your marble ball carrier stay on the zipline as it goes from the top to the bottom?
3. What kinds of materials should be in contact with the zipline so that the carrier slides quickly?

CREATE (25 minutes):

Use the supplies to build your marble ball carrier. Then make the zipline using the fishing line. You can run the line between the back of a chair and a stack of books. Make sure the high end is about two to three feet above the low end. Now test the carrier by inserting it on the line. Your design may not work as planned when you test it the first time. Study the problems and then redesign. For example, if your marble ball carrier:

Keeps dropping the ball, check that it has a big enough place to hold the ball.

Stops partway down, make sure there's nothing blocking your carrier where it touches the line.

Doesn't balance well, adjust the weights. Add weights or move them so they are further below the zipline. This changes the carrier's center of gravity, the point within an object where all parts are in balance with one another. See how changing the numbers and positions of washers or stones affects the carrier's balance.

Takes longer than five seconds to travel the zipline. Find ways to reduce resistance or friction. Friction is the force that resists motion. When you're using something as smooth as fishing line, there should be little friction.

 ## IMPROVE (10 minutes):

Challenge yourself by making a slow version of the carrier. Build a carrier that takes ten seconds to travel the length of the zipline.

Make a carrier that can hold several marbles balls at the same time or it can be multilevel.

 PROJECT EXTENSION:

- Design and create a marble ball carrier that gets to the end of the zipline in 3 seconds.
- Set up two ziplines and race different ball carriers. Measure the time taken, length and height of the ziplines.

Career Introduction: Electrical Engineer

 Engineering connection: Electrical Engineers invent, create, improve and fix electronic devices, tools and equipment. Electrical engineers use lots of math, science and research to develop all kinds of small and large devices and the electrical circuits that help them run.

Grade level: 2-5
Time: 60 minutes

Summary: BristleBots are one variety of the popular moving robot, a simple category of robot controlled by a single vibrating motor.

This BristleBot is made from a toothbrush and a few low-cost materials and can easily be modified for additional challenge.

BRISTLE BOTS

Learning objectives:

- Understand electrical circuits
- Troubleshoot broken connections
- Select materials appropriate for their designs

18

 RELEVANT STANDARDS:

Electricity in circuits can produce light, heat, sound, and magnetic effects. Electrical circuits require a complete loop through which an electrical current can pass. [Grades K – 4]

Some objects occur in nature; others have been designed and made by people to solve human problems and enhance the quality of life. [Grades K – 4]

Electrical circuits provide a means of transferring electrical energy when heat, light, sound, and chemical changes are produced.

Communicate a problem, design, and solution. Student abilities should include oral, written, and

pictorial communication of the design process and product. [Grades K – 4]

International Technology Education Association

The Nature of Technology 1,2

Technology and Society 6

Design 8,9,10

Abilities of the Technological World

The Nature of Technology 1,2

Technology and Society 6

Design 8,9,10

Abilities of the Technological World

 ## Materials:

A toothbrush with even, angled bristles
A vibrating pager motor with wires/other tiny motor with an unbalanced output shaft with wires
Foam tape
An alkaline or lithium coin cell or watch battery (1.5 V or 3 V)

With the Students:

 ## ASK (5 min):

Pique interest by asking, "What is a bristle bot? How do you make a bristle bot? . Tell students that Electrical Engineers invent, create, improve and fix electronic devices, tools and equipment. Electrical engineers use lots of math, science and research to develop all kinds of small and large devices and the electrical circuits that help them run. Today we are going to make a bristle bot.

IMAGINE (10 min):

Have students discuss what are the important parts of these Birstlebots? (Toothbrush heads, motors, coin battery.).

Brainstorm some designs. How could you make the bristle move? How do you stick the motor on the brush head? Where deos the battery go? How do you place the battery? How do you make the connections? Can there be sany switch?

PLAN (10 minutes):

Have kids plan out and discuss how they would make the bristle bot. Ask them to sketch their designs on a piece of paper or in their design notebooks. The starting point is, of course, the toothbrush. A good one has uniformly angled bristles. If the bristle length is nonuniform, it may take scissors to make the bristles all the same. Cut off the handle of the toothbrush, leaving only a neat little robotics platform.

Next, a vibrating pager motor or other tiny motor with an unbalanced output shaft is needed.

The kind used for this example run on almost any common voltage: probably a range of 1-9 V. As a power source, use an alkaline or lithium coin cell or watch battery, either 1.5 V or 3 V.

The last substantial ingredient is foam tape, used to hold the motor in place atop the toothbrush robotic platform.

CREATE (25 minutes):

1. Cut off the handle of the toothbrush to produce the robotics platform.
2. Stick foam tape the size of the toothbrush head to hold the motor in place.
3. Attach the motor to the foam tape. The tape provides a spacer so that the rotating weight does not hit the toothbrush head. It also provides a strong, flexible connection to the base that is able to handle the severe vibration that this robot experiences.
4. Now for the battery, do not stand the battery on end, as it will be insecure and fall off easily. Instead, bend one of the wires from the motor and stick it to the foam, so that you can stick the battery to the foam tape, as well, and still make an electrical connection.
5. Connect the other wire on the other side of the battery, and the motor can run.

👍 IMPROVE (10 minutes):

Discuss what happened.
Refinements: The completed BristleBot is now running and ready for action. When it is set down, it may tend to steer left or right.

Battery and motor placement, bristle shape, and even one stray bristle can interfere with the motion. Encourage students to experiment with each of these elements, to get their Bristlebot to run straight. Motor rotation direction can also influence the behavior, so it may help to flip the battery upside down.

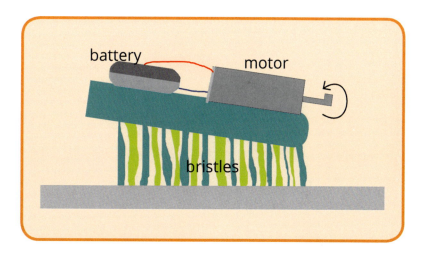

Once the BristleBot is going straight, it will continue on until it hits something, which will turn it and send it off in another direction. Several BristleBots can race across a room at once, creating a fun group activity

Then, challenge them to consider and devise, design modifications. What would happen if the toothbrush bristles were not straight? What could be done to the BristleBot to make it go in circles? Could a similar bristlebot be made from a flat-topped dust broom or a hair comb?

Career Introduction: Chemical Engineer

 Engineering connection: Chemical engineers use chemistry, physics and math along with engineering tools to solve problems relating to the production and use of chemicals. This includes things like purifying drinking water, treating waste, improving medicines, treatments and producing and processing food.

Grade level: 1-5
Time: 60 minutes

Summary: Matter exists in three states: solid, liquid and gas, but sometimes a substance does not seem to fit in any of these categories. Is clay or slime, a solid or a liquid?
In this activity, you will make slime and have fun investigating its behavior. You can stretch and pull it or break it into pieces. You may be able to bounce it.

BOUNCY CLAY

Learning objectives:

Students will identify the properties of solids, liquids, gases and colloids. Understand similarities and differences between colloids and solids, liquids and gasses.
Students make bouncy clay (a colloid) and use the scientific method to experiment with its properties.

RELEVANT STANDARDS:

NATIONAL SCIENCE EDUCATION STANDARDS

Materials:

Elmer's Glue-All
Sta-Flo Concentrated Starch
Set Of Measuring Spoons
Plastic Wrap
Plastic Cups
Popsicle Sticks
(Optional) Food Color
(Optional) Small Plastic Bags

With the Students:

ASK (5 min):

Get students interested by telling them that chemical engineers use chemistry, physics and math along with engineering tools to solve problems relating to the production and use of chemicals. This includes things like purifying drinking water, treating waste, improving medicines, treatments and producing and processing food. Today they are going to be chemical engineers and make a funny slime.

IMAGINE (10 min):

Have students imagine and discuss the properties of solids, liquids and gas. Although matter exists in these three states: solid, liquid and gas, sometimes a substance does not behave according to any of these categories. A substance may behave or have characteristics of more than one of these states. Some materials like asphalt and lead initially act like a solid, but over long periods of time they begin to act like a fluid.

(According to grade) Explain that colloids are mixtures of a substance suspended in another substance. The suspended materials are so tiny, only 1 to 100 nanometers (10^{-9} meters) long, that they do not sink to the bottom of the other substance. Materials like colloids resist small stresses but yield (move) with large stresses and begin to flow like fluids. Some examples of colloids are smoke (solid particles suspended in air), fog, mayonnaise, toothpaste and the funny putty that you will make in this lesson.

In 1678, Sir Isaac Newton formulated a law which describes the movement of fluids when a shearing force is applied (a shearing force occurs when you slide one thing over another). Today, scientists refer to liquids and gases which move according to that law as Newtonian fluids. For Newtonian fluids, the change in velocity is proportional to the amount of shear stress. Common liquids and gases which are Newtonian include water, oil, mercury, gasoline, alcohol, air, helium, hydrogen and steam.

Fluids which do not follow that law are called non-Newtonian. An example of a non-Newtonian fluid is toothpaste, which does not flow out of the tube until a certain amount of force is applied by squeezing – not just any little force. You know from experience that if you squeeze a toothpaste tube just a little bit, the toothpaste will not come out. The funny putty you make in this activity is an example of a non-Newtonian colloid. It takes a firm pull to make the funny putty stretch. What happens if you pull the funny putty very quickly? Does it break in two? Scientists and engineers need to understand colloid behavior to produce or manufacture plastics, rubber, detergent, paint, food products and paper. Even environmental scientists learn colloid behavior and how it affects fog, precipitation and soils.

📄 PLAN (10 minutes):

Look at your materials and think through how you can use them to make funny slime. Predict what ratio and portions will give you the best results.

✋ CREATE (25 minutes):

Cut an 10 inch piece of plastic wrap and place it on the table in front of you. You will use this to knead the slime. Later you will wrap your funny slime with this plastic wrap so that it does not dry out. Measure the starch and glue and pour them into separate small cups. Use twice as much starch (for example, measure 1 teaspoon of starch and 1/2 teaspoon of glue; or measure 1 tablespoon starch and 1 1/2 teaspoons of glue).

You may have to experiment with the measurements – the drier the slime is, the easier it will form a ball and bounce on a hard surface. Pour the starch into the glue. You can add a drop of food color. Stir the mixture with a popsicle stick.
Keep stirring till the mixture firms. You can remove it from the cup, place it on the plastic wrap and use your hands to mix your slime.

👍 IMPROVE (10 minutes):

Now have some fun! Try out these properties to see if your funny putty behaves this way. If you pull the putty slowly, does it stretch? If you pull it quickly, does it break? Does it bounce off hard surfaces?

If the putty is left exposed to air, it will become brittle. Wrap your putty in the plastic wrap or a small plastic bag.

PROJECT EXTENSION:

If you use other types of glue, the slime properties may not be the same.

You can use the worksheet to record how different glues affect the slime. Can you make a magnetic slime or a glow-in-the dark one?

Career Introduction: Civil Engineer

 Engineering connection: Civil engineers design and build infrastructure like bridges, dams, buildings, and tunnels. They also work with the construction of house and water networks, irrigation and sewerage networks.

Grade level: 1-5
Time: 60 minutes

Summary: Students will build a table out of tubes of newspaper that is strong enough to hold a heavy book. They will learn to brainstorm, test, evaluate, and redesign their tables to support more weight and figure out how to keep the table legs from buckling.

STURDY PAPER TABLE

Learning objectives:

1) Work in cooperative groups or alone to construct a table using materials provided.
2) Discuss what happened, how they solved problems that arose, what strategies they used, and why certain arrangements of materials proved stronger than others.

RELEVANT STANDARDS:

Massachusetts Curriculum Frameworks, Science and Technology/Engineering Standards
Materials and Tools 1.1-1.2; Engineering Design 2.1-2.3; Physical Science 1.
ITEA The Nature of Technology
National Science Standards; Science as Inquiry; Properties of Materials; Technology Design.

Materials:

Newspaper sheets (8 per person)
Cardboard or particle board (one 8.5x 11inches piece per person)
Masking tape
Books or stacks of magazines to test each table's strength
Paper or design notebooks for sketching table designs
Ruler to measure height of table

With the Students:

ASK (5 min):

Get students interested by asking, "Do you think you can build a table out of newspaper?". Tell students that civil engineers design and build infrastructure like bridges, dams, buildings, and tunnels. They also work with the construction of house and water networks, irrigation and sewerage networks. Today they will have to build a structure like civil engineers.

IMAGINE (10 min):

Have students imagine and discuss how a thin piece of newspaper will be able to hold the weight of books. Have them look at the furniture in the room and find out how different supports they see can prevent tables and chairs from tilting or twisting.

Show students how to make a strong tube by rolling newspapers tightly. Start at one corner and roll diagonally toward the other corner, with the first roll about the diameter of a straw. Tape the tube closed with a strip or two of tape–and wave it around to show how stiff and strong it is.

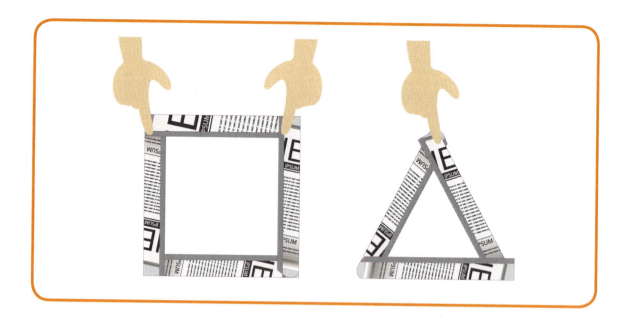

Hint: To avoid having to spend time teaching each student how to make a tube out of newspaper, make samples ready in advance and show them. For instance, take three pieces of newspaper. Use one to show how tight the first roll needs to be to make it strong. Roll the second paper halfway up. With the third, show a finished tube. Students can feel the three tubes and try to understand which one is the strongest.

Show different shapes made from the tubes. Take two newspaper tubes; bend one into a triangle, a common shape for supports, and the other into a square. Tape them closed and set them on the floor. Push down on them and rock them from side to side.

The triangle will be able to withstand more force and provide more stability than the square, but orientation matters! A triangle resting on its point will be weaker and less stable than before.

PLAN (10 minutes):

Have kids plan out how they want to design the table structure. Have students brainstorm how they could use these materials to make a paper table that's at least 8 inches tall and strong enough to hold a book. Ask them to sketch their designs on a piece of paper or in their design notebooks.

CREATE (25 minutes):

Now have the kids begin building. Ask questions to encourage students to think about how they might solve any design problems. Some could be:
- The table legs tilt or twist. (Support the legs by running tubes between them.)
- A tube buckles when loaded down. (Roll loose tubes tighter. Tape securely. Reinforce or replace dented or wrinkled areas that weaken legs.)
- The table wobbles. (Make sure it isn't lopsided and has adequate supports. Reduce height to increase stability.)
- The table collapses. (Check that the base is truly sturdy. In general, the more triangles kids use, the stronger their tables will be.)

IMPROVE (10 minutes):

Discuss what happened. Have kids talk about their designs. Discuss how they solved any problems that came up. Ask how they were able to support a heavy book on just pieces of newspaper. How did changing the shape support more weight?

Tubes distribute the load thereby increasing the amount of weight that paper can support. How did knowing certain arrangements of materials, like triangles, influence the table's design? What helped make a table especially strong? Students may mention the use of good bracing, triangles, and keeping everything compact.

 PROJECT EXTENSION:

Build a table that can hold two or more heavy books.
Build a taller table and chairs to go with the table.

Career Introduction: Acoustical Engineer

 Engineering connection: Acoustical engineers help design high quality sports stadiums, recording studios, auditoriums and other spaces so that everyone in the audience can hear the quality of music that is being produced. To do that, they must understand music and the frequencies at which different notes are formed.

Grade level: 1-5
Time: 30 minutes

Summary: Students in grades 1 – 5 work with partners to investigate sound frequencies and acoustical engineering by creating a simple musical instrument: Guitar

Learning objectives:

After this activity, students should be able to:
1. Understand the connection between sound waves and frequency.
2. Understand that high frequencies produce high-pitched sounds and low frequencies produce low-pitched sounds.

RELEVANT STANDARDS:

International Technology and Engineering Educators Association: D. Tools, materials, and skills are used to make things and carry out tasks. Various relationships exist between technology and other fields of study.

Next Generation Science Standards: Develop a model of waves to describe patterns in terms of amplitude and wavelength and that waves can cause objects to move.

Materials:

Sturdy shoebox
8-10 rubber bands of varying widths
Pencil
Instrument Construction Worksheet

Procedure:

This is a fairly unstructured activity; be sure to give students plenty of time to experiment and explore their instruments. If you like, bring in an electric tuner so that students can investigate the frequencies their instruments are creating. There is also a free, easy-to-use tuner app available for smartphones called gStrings Free. Make a sample musical instrument to show the class before the activity begins.

With the Students:

ASK (5 min):

Get them interested by telling them about acoustical engineers. Tell students that they help design high quality sports stadiums, recording studios, auditoriums and other spaces so that everyone in the audience can hear the good quality music that is being produced. To do that, they must understand music and the frequencies at which different notes are formed.

IMAGINE (10 min):

To know more about sound, students need to build an instrument, a guitar. Explain that sound is energy that moves through a medium (for example, air) in a wave pattern.

It's time to create your own musical instruments. We know that different notes have different frequencies. Remember, while you are making them, I want you to think about the different frequencies your instrument is creating. The frequency of a sound is directly related to its pitch. That is, the more waves per second hitting your ear, the higher in pitch the tone is and subsequently, the smaller the wavelength. (Draw it on the board)

PLAN (10 minutes):

Ask yourself if the sounds your instrument makes have high or low frequencies. And make sure to check out some of the other instruments – they all are going to sound a little different! See if you can figure out what some of the differences are.

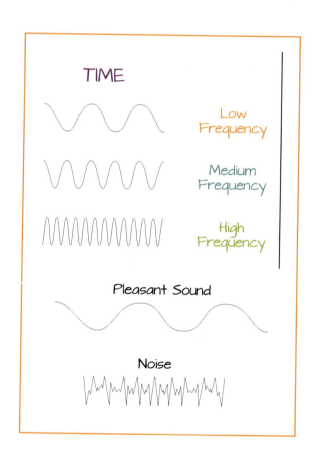

One more thing you should know before you begin: Sometimes, when we hear a sound, it sounds really good to our ears, like beautiful music. Other times, it sounds like a horrible noise.

The sound waves for a pleasant sound and a noisy sound look very different – does anyone have an idea about how they might look? The pleasant sound wave is very smooth, like this (draw it on the board) while the noisy sound wave is rough, like this (draw it on the board). The noisy wave actually looks noisy, doesn't it? (see Figure for these two waves.)

CREATE (25 minutes):

Divide the class into teams of two students each.
Have teams spend a few minutes deciding how they wish to build their project.
Hand out the worksheets.
Provide groups with the materials for their instruments.
Direct students to begin designing and creating their instruments.
Help with construction when necessary.
Once students have completed their instruments, give them time to practice playing them.

👍 IMPROVE (10 minutes): Investigating questions:

Ask students questions regarding the frequency of the created sounds. For example: Do you think that your guitar is making high or low frequency sounds? (Reminder: higher frequency sounds are higher pitch sounds, while slower frequency sounds are the lower sounds.) How can you improve the guitar's sound? How many different kinds of instruments are in an orchestra? What does an acoustical engineer do?

📁 PROJECT EXTENSION:

As you assist students with creating their instruments, ask them what they are learning about frequency. Have students learn about engineers who are instrumental in the music industry

Career Introduction: NASA Scientist

 Engineering connection: NASA is one of the largest employers of engineers in the world. This activity has hands-on engineering and the adventure of space exploration for students. The activity is related to NASA's Lunar Reconnaissance Orbiter and NASA's Lunar Crater Observation and Sensing Satellite missions.

Grade level: 3-5
Time: 60 minutes

Summary: In this lesson, students will play the role of NASA aerospace engineers. They design and build a moon lander with a shock-absorbing system that protects two marshmallow "astronauts" when they land.

NASA SCIENTIST: Lunar Lander

Learning objectives:

Design and build a shock-absorbing system out of paper, straws and mini-marshmallows.
Attach their shock absorber to a cardboard platform.
Improve their design.

RELEVANT STANDARDS:

National Science Education Standards
International Technology Education Association Content Standards
Massachusetts Science and Technology/Engineering Standards
National Council of Teachers of Mathematics Standards

Materials:

1 piece of stiff paper or cardboard (approximately 4 x 5 in/10 x 13 cm)
1 small paper or plastic cup
3 index cards (3 x 5 in/8 x 13 cm)
2 regular marshmallows
10 miniature marshmallows
3 rubber bands
8 plastic straws
Scissors
Tape

With the Students:

ASK (5 min):

Get them excited by talking about NASA's space adventures and scientists. Explain to students why a spacecraft that can land gently is important for getting astronauts to and from the moon safely. Today they are going to build a safe moon lander- Lunar Lander just like NASA scientists

IMAGINE (10 min):

Landing on the moon is tricky. First, since a spacecraft can go as fast as 18,000 miles per hour (29,000 km/hour) on its way to the moon, it needs to slow way down. Then it needs to land gently. NASA is looking for safe landing sites on the moon. Once they find one, they need to design and build a spacecraft that can land there without injuring astronauts or damaging the spacecraft.

Today you'll make a lander - a spacecraft that can land safely when you drop it on the floor of the moon – or classroom. As you test your constructed lander, you'll find ways to make it work better. Improving a design based on testing is an important part of the engineering design process.

Demonstrate a spring made out of an index card and Divide the class into small groups and distribute the materials.

📄 PLAN (10 minutes):

What kind of shock absorber can you make from these materials to help soften a landing? (Mini-marshmallows can serve as soft footpads. Cards can be folded into springs. Straws can provide a flexible structure. Rubber bands can flex and hold things together.)

How will you make sure the lander doesn't tip over as it falls through the air? (Making the parts below the platform weigh more than the parts on the top helps the lander fall straight down. Also, it helps to evenly distribute the weight on top of the platform.)

CREATE (25 minutes):

First, design a shock-absorbing system from the supplied materials. Then, put your spacecraft together. Attach the shock absorbers to the cardboard platform. Finally, add a cabin for the astronauts. Tape the cup to the platform. Put two astronauts (the large marshmallows) in it. The cup has to stay open.

TEST: Ready to test? Drop your lander from a height of one foot (30 cm). *Note: Teachers may direct students to test their landers in their individual groups. Or, in a smaller class, each group can demonstrate before the class while the other students watch and make notes about the different design solutions and outcomes.

👍 IMPROVE (10 minutes): Investigating questions:

If the "astronauts" bounce out, figure out ways to improve your design. Study any problems and redesign. For example, if your spacecraft:

1. Tips over as it falls through the air - make sure it's level when you release it. Also check that the cup is centered on the cardboard. Finally, check that the weight is evenly distributed.
2. Bounces the astronauts out of the cup - add soft pads or change the number or position of the shock absorbers. Also, make the springs less springy so they don't bounce the astronauts out.

 PROJECT EXTENSION:

Hold a "How High Can You Go?" contest. Have kids drop their landers from two feet. Eliminate all landers that bounce out their "astronauts." Next, raise the height to three feet. Test springs of different sizes. Have kids see if the number of folds in an index card makes a difference in the amount of force the spring can absorb.

Career Introduction: Toy Designer

 Engineering connection: Toy designers work in a toy designing firm. They develop and design products such as cars and children's toys using variety of materials, for example plastic, vinyl, wood, metal, latex and resin. They need to create products that are attractive and functional for the user.

Grade level: 1-5
Time: 60 minutes

Summary: In "Simple Slingshot" students explore slingshot designs. When work in teams of "engineers" to design and build their own marshmallow slingshot out of everyday items. They test their slingshot, evaluate their results and present to the class.

TOY DESIGNER: SLINGSHOT

Learning objectives:

Designed and constructed a slingshot
Measured distance and calculated speed (as per grade)
Tested and refined their designs
Communicated their design process and results

RELEVANT STANDARDS:

National Science Education Standards

Massachusetts Curriculum Frameworks, Science and Technology/Engineering Standards:

Materials:

2 toilet-paper tubes (or 1 paper-towel tube, cut in half)
Tape
Single-hole punch (optional)
Stubby pencil
Pen or marker
2 thin rubber bands
Scissors
Marshmallow (or small ball)

With the Students:

ASK (5 min):

Get students interested by telling them that a toy designer works in a toy designing firm. They develop and design products, such as cars and children's toys using a variety of materials, like plastic, vinyl, wood, metal, latex and resin. They need to create products that are attractive and functional for the user.

Today the students are going to be toy designers and make a marshmallow slingshot.

IMAGINE (10 min):

Have students imagine and discuss what a slingshot is. How is a slingshot made? Have them look at some images of slingshots, or videos of slingshot games. That way they have better understanding of the design activity.

Have you ever jumped on a trampoline? When you push the trampoline's surface down, you store energy in the springs. Stored energy is called potential energy. You go flying back up when the stored energy changes to motion energy (called kinetic energy). In your slingshot, pulling the plunger back increases the rubber band's potential energy. Let go and the potential energy turns into kinetic energy—the marshmallow goes flying. Bows and arrows and shock absorbers on a bike use potential and kinetic energy to work.

PLAN (10 minutes):

Look at your materials and decide how you can use them to build a slingshot. Then sketch your ideas on a piece of paper or in your design notebook.
1. Using these materials, what kind of slingshot can you make?
2. How will you use the 2 toilet tubes? Can one be made into a plunger, i.e the inner tube?
3. How can the rubber bands help?

CREATE (25 minutes):

Use the supplies to build your slingshot.
Make the plunger (i.e., the inner tube) by cutting a toilet-paper tube in half, lengthwise.
Then squeeze it so it's about half its original diameter and tape it.
Punch two holes and insert the pencil through the holes
Cut slits: take the second toilet-paper tube. Draw two short lines straight down from the rim, about as far apart as the width of your index finger.
Make two slits by cutting each line. Do this again at the same end of the tube, opposite your first set of slits.
Attach the rubber bands. Push a rubber band into one set of slits. Be gentle. Avoid bending the piece of cardboard between the slits.
Do the same on the other side. (Thin rubber bands work best because they fit into the slits without bending the cardboard too much.)
Assemble the blaster
Slide the plunger into the larger tube (called the "grip").
Hook each rubber band around a pencil end • Load a marshmallow. It should rest on top of the plunger.
Now blast it across the room!

 ## IMPROVE (10 minutes):

Instead of using a toilet paper tube to make the plunger, use a paper-towel tube. This will give you a longer pull, which will stretch the rubber bands more, thus increasing their potential energy. How far can you shoot a marshmallow?

 PROJECT EXTENSION:

Invent more games. How many paper cups can you knock over?
How accurate are you when launching marshmallows into a set of cups?

MAKER SHOWCASE

Synthesize knowledge and produce a final collection of projects from the above projects. Plan, design and use a process to make creative tech or to synchronize all these together into a unified model. Demonstrate appropriate safety procedures. Use engineering processes to develop this unified project.

Now that you have completed all nine lesson plans it is time for the last activity – the Maker Showcase.

You are required to present your work to the group. Ensure that you have all your notes and project models neatly prepared. Read through all the lessons again, ensuring that you understand your work fully. You will be asked questions and expected to demonstrate the engineering principles that you have learned.

Join the WIZKIDS CLUB

Enter today and win a FREE BOOK!

Do you have any travel adventure stories or project ideas you want share with me? Yes? Great! You can mail me at my id and become a member of the WIZKIDS CLUB!

www.wizkidsclub.com

Write to me at: sumita@wizkidsclub.com

Made in the USA
San Bernardino, CA
14 November 2018